THE
PEOPLE'S
CHOICE

Also by Alvin Schwartz

The Night Workers
What Do You Think? *An Introduction to Public Opinion*
The City and Its People
Museum: *The Story of America's Treasure Houses*

THE
PEOPLE'S
CHOICE

The Story of Candidates, Campaigns, and Elections

By Alvin Schwartz

illustrated with photographs

E. P. DUTTON & COMPANY, INC.   NEW YORK

All of you will, in a sense, hold office
in the Great Republic....
JOHN F. KENNEDY

Contents

There are in the United States more than a half-million jobs that must be filled every few years through elections. The most important, of course, are those of President and Vice President. The people also must elect 50 governors, 100 United States Senators, and 435 Representatives. In addition, they must choose lawmakers for each town, city, county, and state, plus judges, sheriffs, tax collectors, members of school boards and library boards, and many other officials as well.

The men and women who win these elections manage our government for us, making decisions that affect our lives in a thousand ways. Their decisions determine how good our schools are, how safe we are from criminals, how clean the air is, how crowded the highways are, how much we pay in taxes. At the very highest levels of government, they help decide whether there is peace or war.

Each year hundreds of thousands of men and women run for office. Many are fascinated by government and want a chance to serve their fellow citizens in this way. Others are attracted by the power, prestige, and salary they might gain. Whatever their reasons for running, there are important stakes involved, for the outcome affects how well our affairs are handled. This is as true of a race for town council as it is of a nationwide contest for the Presidency.

To understand a political campaign, it is important to understand many things: how the candidates came to be chosen, what their beliefs are on important matters, what changes they propose if they are elected, how they organize and conduct their campaigns, how they pay the costs involved, who their supporters are, and, finally, why one wins over another. In every case the place to start is with the political parties.

$\mathbf{A}$ political party is an organization whose members tend to share many of the same ideas on important public questions. It has but one reason for being: to win control of the government so that its members can put their ideas into effect. In some countries a party may seize power by force. In the United States a party tries to obtain control by naming candidates for office, then working to elect them.

George Washington felt that parties would divide the country rather than unite it and advised against their formation. Yet even while he was in office differences of opinion developed over how government affairs should be handled, and the nation's first parties began to take shape. One was the Federalist Party which represented

12

the interests of merchants, bankers, and other businessmen in the northeastern states. It was led by Alexander Hamilton, the man on the left. The other was the Democratic-Republican Party, led by Thomas Jefferson, which worked in behalf of farmers in the South and along the frontier.

Within 25 years the Federalists had lost their following and disbanded. The Democratic-Republicans, on the other hand, fought among themselves. Then, in the 1820's they split into two factions from which today's major parties were to grow.

One group, led by Andrew Jackson, formed the Democratic Party. Its supporters were largely farmers and frontiersmen. The other group, led by Henry Clay and Daniel Webster, organized the National Republican Party, which later became known as the Whigs. Its supporters included many businessmen and other property owners. When the Whigs argued among themselves and finally disbanded in the 1850's, the Republican Party replaced them. The chart below shows these changes.

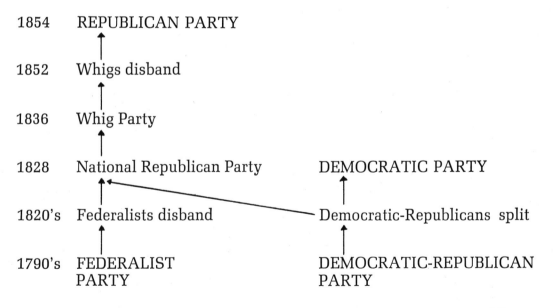

What is the difference between today's Republicans and Democrats? The Republican elephant and the Democratic donkey, created a century ago, still are an amusing way of telling them apart. But, of course, there are other differences that are more important in understanding the two parties.

One involves their supporters. Although both try to appeal to as many voters as possible, much of their support comes from certain groups. The Republicans draw many votes from businessmen, professional men, and farmers, and from people who live in suburbs and small towns. The Democrats rely heavily on workingmen, members of minority groups, and others who live in cities.

14

The parties also tend to differ in their approaches to government, particularly national government. The Republicans generally have been the more conservative, often moving quite cautiously when it comes to spending money or otherwise using government power. The Democrats generally are the more liberal, showing more willingness to make changes.

By and large this is the way the parties have behaved for many years. But they cover such a vast country that these are not the approaches all Republicans or Democrats use. Many Democratic candidates in the South, for example, are conservatives, while some Republicans in the North are liberals. However, this does not concern party officials a great deal, especially at election time. Their major interest in a candidate is not so much his viewpoint but whether he can win.

15

Norman Thomas, Socialist Party

J. Strom Thurmond, States Rights Party

Along with the Republicans and Democrats, there are many small parties, or third parties as they are known, that run candidates for office. Each of the men on this page and the next was a small party's candidate for President. Not one had the slightest chance of winning, but to make their ideas known they ran anyway.

Over the years these parties have included Know Nothings, Populists, Socialists, Progressives, Communists, Conservatives, Prohibitionists, Vegetarians, and scores of others. Some are concerned with advancing just one idea. The Prohibitionists, for example, are opposed to the sale of alcoholic beverages. Others, just like the major parties, are interested in broader changes. Many small parties exist only for one or two elections, forming in response to a particular issue, then disappearing. A few, like the Socialists and Prohibitionists, have been in operation for many years.

16

In some cases the candidates of small parties do very well in an election. Presidential candidates have polled over a million votes. Moreover, those who run for state or local office occasionally win. Bridgeport, Connecticut, and Milwaukee, Wisconsin, both have had Socialist mayors in recent years.

But far more often there are few votes and no victories. The 1960 Presidential election was typical. In that race John Kennedy and Richard Nixon together polled 68 million votes. The 12 other candidates, all from small parties, together got 500,000. Not only are such men badly defeated at the polls, they may be ridiculed and physically attacked for their ideas. In this photograph of Henry Wallace, one can see the vegetables and eggs unfair persons in the audience threw at him because they felt his views were too extreme.

Of what value are small parties? Their great contribution is ideas for programs that might benefit the country. Some of these ideas are worthless, but when a useful one begins to attract votes usually the Republicans or Democrats will make it their own.

Henry Wallace, Progressive Party

17

Shortly before this was written the Gallup Poll asked adults through-out the country about their political beliefs. Were they Republicans or Democrats? Or were they Independents who shifted from party to party, depending on the candidates and the issues? This is what was found.

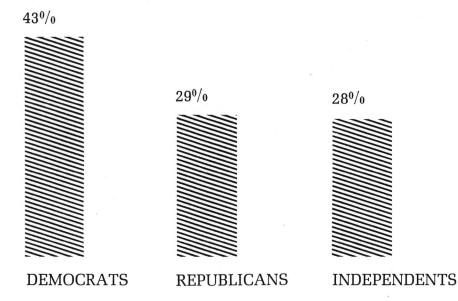

43%

29%

28%

DEMOCRATS   REPUBLICANS   INDEPENDENTS

Although the pollsters regularly ask the public about its political beliefs, the answers have not varied greatly in years. Usually one person in two says he is a Democrat and one in four says he is a Republican. The remainder say they are Independents or, in a small number of cases, that they support a third party. In some sections there are far more Republicans than Democrats. As we have seen,

18

often this is so in suburbs and rural areas. Otherwise it is generally the Democrats who are in the majority.

This is a serious problem for the Republicans. It means that to win many elections, including Presidential elections, they must attract the votes of a sizable number of Independents and Democrats. When they have the right candidate or the right issue, occasionally this happens. It was only with such support, for example, that the Republican Dwight Eisenhower was elected President in 1952 and 1956.

For many years the Republicans were the majority party. From 1860 to 1928 they elected 14 out of 18 Presidents. Should conditions change in the country or should the parties change in some way, this could happen again.

If you don't already know, it would be interesting to ask your parents which party they favor and what their reasons are. Many people favor one party instead of another because they believe in approaches or programs that party has supported over the years. Others support a party because of tradition. They live in a section where almost everyone backs the same party, or they vote the way they do because their parents voted that way. By the time a boy or girl is your age, he already may have political ideas like those of his parents.

At times, however, there are other influences. If a voter is out of work, if food prices have gotten very high, if there is rioting in the cities, or if a war continues without any end in sight, he may ignore his traditions or forget what a party has done in the past and turn to the party that seems at the moment to have the best solution.

A political party actually is a collection of thousands of parties operating on their own in towns, cities, counties, and states. Each is concerned with electing candidates to office in its area. In an election for a higher office, all concerned are expected to work together. The Democrats and the Republicans have such party units throughout the country, from neighborhood groups to a national committee. This diagram shows how the major parties are organized.

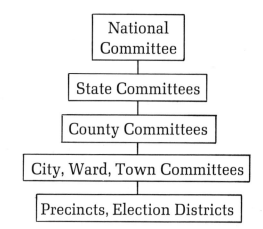

The precincts or election districts at the bottom are small neighborhood areas, usually with from 500 to 1,000 voters each. Every city and every town is divided into such units. If you live in a city, it first may have been divided into wards, then into precincts. In all, there are over 170,000 precincts throughout the country. Each party tries to have a leader, or captain, plus several workers in each one. Their job is to increase the number of party supporters, campaign for their

20

party's candidates, and on Election Day be sure that everyone who can help the party casts his ballot.

All the precinct leaders in a town, ward, or city also are members of a committee that operates their local party. All the local parties are then represented on a county committee that operates the county party. In turn, each of the county parties has representatives on a state committee that oversees operation of the state party. Finally, the state parties have members who serve on a national committee that conducts the party's affairs at that level, such as the Democratic National Committee below.

Each of these party units is headed by a leader or a chairman. The larger units also have paid staffs to carry out their work, but others depend on volunteers. In fact, one of your parents or someone on your street may be a volunteer party worker. How successful a party is in electing its candidates depends a good deal on how strong an organization it has—whether there are active units everywhere and whether they work together.

For all their importance, political organizations have a poor reputation. People tend to think of them as powerful, selfish groups that dictate who a party's candidates will be, then help them to win, and in return expect government jobs, the "right" votes on certain issues, and other favors. Political organizations that operate in this way are known as "machines." The men who run them are called "bosses."

At times the people have good reason to be concerned about "machines." The men below, for example, were two of the most successful bosses in modern times, controlling the government in their cities for years. Today, bosses and machines still operate in many places. There are big-city bosses, in fact, whose organizations are so strong that men who want to be candidates for President often seek their help.

However, there also are political organizations that are run in a more democratic fashion and take the needs of the people into account to a greater extent. One finds such groups where people are interested enough in their government to join a party and participate in its work. Only when politics is left to but a few politicians do bosses appear and machines grow.

Frank Hague of Jersey City *James Curley of Boston*

The parties stand at the center of the political stage. Clustered about them are thousands of organizations with a deep interest in their candidates.

There are political clubs that work the year round in behalf of a party. Some are open to any adult who lives in a particular area. Others are for women or for young adults. There also are two kinds of clubs for high-school students, the Teen Dems and the Teen-Age Republicans.*

Then there are "citizens' organizations" such as Volunteers for Johnson-Humphrey and Citizens for Nixon-Lodge. These are set

*For membership information write to the following addresses: Teen Dems, Young Democrats Division, Democratic National Committee, 2600 Virginia Avenue, N.W., Washington, D.C.; Teen-Age Republicans, 1010 Vermont Avenue, N.W., Washington, D.C.

up to give Independents and others a chance to work for a candidate they like without having to support his party, which they otherwise may oppose.

In addition, there are pressure groups such as labor unions, business associations, and farm and veterans' organizations that may decide which candidates will help them the most and work for their election.

Finally, there are civic groups that provide information on candidates and issues and encourage people to vote. These include the League of Women Voters and the American Heritage Foundation.

A person who decides to run for office must travel a long road from the day he makes his decision to Election Day. First, he must win his party's nomination. If he succeeds, he must spend many weeks campaigning against the candidates of other parties. In the end, after months of effort, he may win—or he may not.

In many states the parties begin selecting their candidates a half year or more before the elections. In the earliest stages the party leaders decide which men and women they would like to see nominated. In each case they try to find somone who has had experience in government, is known to the voters, and has a pleasant personality and appearance. The color of a man's skin and the church he attends also may be of importance since, unfortunately, these things sometimes affect how people vote. Finally, there is the question of money. If a person is able to pay for the cost of a campaign, he is that much more attractive to the politicians.

Meanwhile, other persons may decide they want the party's nomination even though the leaders do not support them.

The party's members then make the final choice. In some states they do so at a nominating convention at which delegates who represent them cast ballots. More often the decision is made in a primary election in which all the party's supporters can vote. It is a simple matter for someone to get his name on the ballot. All he must do is obtain the signatures of a certain number of party members who back him.

Often, however, there is no opposition to the leaders' candidates, and a convention or a primary is a quiet affair. When there is a contest, the rivals may conduct costly campaigns to get the votes they need to be nominated.

Personal Choice	Procedure for write in voting		COLUMN 1 REPUBLICAN	COLUMN 2 REPUBLICAN	COLUMN 3 DEMOCRATIC	COLUMN 4 DEMOCRATIC
		1				Cease Fire Vietnam; Jersey Democratic Council DAVID FROST
		2	For United States Senator (VOTE FOR ONE)			Democrats Against Sales Tax JOHN J. WINBERRY
		3				Integrity, Honesty, Representation, Creativity, Science, Progress JERRY CHARLES BURMEISTER
		4	CLIFFORD P. CASE		Regular Democratic Organization WARREN W. WILENTZ	No War No Sales Tax Democrats CLARENCE COGGINS
		5	For Member of House of Representatives (Fourth Congressional District) (VOTE FOR ONE) — Regular Organization Republican RALPH CLARK CHANDLER		Regular Democratic Organization FRANK THOMPSON, Jr.	
		6	For Sheriff (VOTE FOR ONE) — Regular Organization Republican HORACE A. READING		Regular Democratic Organization JOSEPH S. HOLLAND	
		7	For Surrogate (VOTE FOR ONE) — Regular Organization Republican ROGER W. YARD		Regular Democratic Organization JOHN E. CURRY	
		8	For Members of the Board of Chosen Freeholders (VOTE FOR TWO) — Regular Organization Republican KARL WEIDEL		Regular Democratic Organization THOMAS J. WARWICK	
		9	Regular Organization Republican CLIFFORD W. SNEDEKER		Regular Democratic Organization BENJAMIN L. PALUMBO	
		10	For Members of Township Committee (VOTE FOR TWO) — Regular Organization Republican JOHN D. WALLACE		Regular Democratic Organization GERALDINE L. BOONE	
		11	Regular Organization Republican DAVID S. THOMPSON		Regular Democratic Organization GEORGE J. GOLDSMITH	
	Procedure for write in voting Push and hold lever below to right, and hold until proper slide is opened	12	For Member of County Committee (Male) (VOTE FOR ONE) — Regular Organization Republican THEODORE H. KENNEDY		Regular Democratic Organization LEROY C. BOLDEN	
		13				
		14	For Member of County Committee (Female) (VOTE FOR ONE) — Regular Organization Republican DOROTHY E. ALEXANDER		Regular Democratic Organization DAISY J. WOOLRIDGE	
		15				
		16	For Coroners (VOTE FOR TWO) — NO PETITION FILED		NO PETITION FILED	FRANCIS P. LARKIN
		17	NO PETITION FILED		NO PETITION FILED	
		18				
		19				

In the primary in which the ballot on the opposite page was used, the only contest involved the Democratic nomination for United States Senator. Four men challenged the leaders' candidate, but failed to defeat him. Of course, a person who does not get his party's nomination can run for office on his own, but his chances of winning would be small.*

At times a primary or a nominating convention is far more important than a general election. This is so in many sections of the South and in other areas where there is only one party with any strength. In such situations a person who wins his party's nomination is certain to win the election. In all others the real fight lies ahead.

The greatest prize a party offers is its nomination for the Presidency. If it already has a President in office and he wishes to run for a second term, the party usually agrees. In other cases, however, winning the nomination can be very difficult.

Each of the major parties makes its decision at a national convention three or four months before the election. Delegates from every state and every territory cast their votes. To win the support of these delegates many men begin campaigning a year or more in advance, often spending millions of dollars in the process. They set up a headquarters, assemble a staff, issue statements on national problems, and travel far and wide making speeches and meeting with delegates and other party leaders.

---

*In some local elections candidates must run on their own, rather than as members of a party. These are called bipartisan elections. A candidate first collects the signatures of a certain number of voters who support him. Then he files these with the government and begins his campaign.

Presidential primaries also may be involved. These are elections in which party members in a state decide which person they favor for the nomination, as these voters in New Hampshire are doing. Fifteen states and the District of Columbia conduct such primaries. In some cases the state's delegates to the national convention then must cast their votes for the winner.

A string of victories in these primaries is a giant step toward the nomination. As a result, candidates may campaign for votes as hard as if they were running for election, as Hubert Humphrey is doing below with the help of his son Greg in a Democratic primary in West Virginia. On the other hand, one or two bad defeats can mean an end to a man's chances.

Because the risk is great and the cost of campaigning is high, not everyone who wants the nomination enters the Presidential primaries. In fact, some avoid them and still are named their party's candidate.

This is a recent Republican national convention. Except for the television and radio networks, it does not look very different from the Republican convention below which took place in Chicago in 1860. At that meeting Abraham Lincoln was nominated for President.

Candidates for President and Vice President have been selected at such meetings since 1832 when the Democrats gathered in Baltimore to nominate Andrew Jackson and Martin Van Buren. Earlier, candidates were nominated by state legislatures and before that by party members who were serving in Congress.

These members of the Kansas delegation are but a few of the 1,300 delegates who attended the Republican convention on the preceding page. Only once every four years do they come together in this way to meet as a national party.

In a single week they conduct the party's business affairs, reach agreement on a platform that describes their beliefs on the issues of the day, select candidates for President and Vice President, and try to unite for the election campaign ahead. If there has been a bitter fight for the nomination, often this is the most difficult task.

Over 15,000 people attend each of the two major conventions. These include the delegates, a substitute or alternate for each delegate, party officials, candidates for the nominations and their supporters, and thousands of newsmen.

31

At times a man wins so much support for the nomination in advance of a convention that he cannot possibly be beaten. But often the fight for the votes of delegates is carried right into the convention hall. Candidates talk with party leaders they think can help and meet with state delegations to plead for their votes. Here Barry Goldwater, in search of the Republican nomination in 1964, answers a question that concerns delegates from Oregon.

32

Meanwhile a candidate's advisers keep close track of how important delegations plan to vote, plotting ways and means of increasing their man's strength. Often the strategy involves a trade: favors or important government jobs for votes. If victory seems within reach, even the nomination for Vice President may be offered to someone who controls the votes that are needed.

As the maneuvering for votes goes on, each of the candidates is officially placed in nomination by a delegate who favors him. Usually this involves a long speech.

Then in each case a great uproar follows

as the candidate's supporters march up and down the aisles accompanied by bands...

and banners...

and pretty girls in costume.

Once the nominations have been made, the balloting begins. First, Alabama is asked how its delegates vote. The chairman of the delegation arises and announces the number of votes each candidate has received. Next Alaska is called, then Arizona, then Arkansas—each state and each territory in turn.

Even as the votes are being announced, a candidate's workers may be on the convention floor bargaining for whatever additional support they can find. If one candidate does not win a majority of votes on the first ballot, the voting begins again, and the bargaining grows more intense.

When at last the Presidential candidate has been named, a candidate for Vice President must be chosen. At times there is a contest, but more often the man who is to run for President indicates whom he wants as a running mate. The delegates vote once more; the two candidates pledge their best efforts; the convention adjourns—and the campaign begins.

What an election campaign is like depends on the office at stake and the number of voters involved. A candidate for a school-board seat may announce he is running by writing a letter to the local paper. He then may make three or four speeches and await the results. But campaigning for office can be far more complicated.

When Mrs. Rowan Boone campaigned for a seat on the town council in Princeton, New Jersey, she had the help of members of the local Democratic organization. In their free time after their jobs, they handled publicity, arranged for advertising, prepared a brochure that told about Mrs. Boone, obtained speaking appearances for her, and raised the money needed to pay for campaign expenses.

When a higher office and a larger area are involved, a candidate is likely to have one or more headquarters and employ a paid staff. In the photograph below, Abraham Beame, left, a candidate for Mayor of New York, meets with members of his staff.

When Ralph Chandler ran for the House of Representatives from New Jersey's Fourth Congressional District, his staff included a manager, an assistant manager, a press agent, a woman who arranged his speaking schedule, a man who drove him from place to place, and a secretary to answer the mail.

He also had other help. Each Sunday the Republican leaders in the four counties where he was campaigning met with his advisers for a strategy session on where he should appear, what he should say, and what he should not say. In addition, he received assistance from the Republican Congressional Campaign Committee, an organization in Washington that helps Republicans running for the House of Representatives. They sent their experts to advise him and installed a teletype machine at his headquarters, over which they provided information for his speeches on national problems and on his opponent's record.

A growing number of candidates also rely on advertising agencies and public-relations firms to create TV programs, radio announcements, and newspaper ads for them. Others pay pollsters to keep track of how they stand with the public. Some even hire organizations that specialize in running a complete campaign, from designing posters and raising money to getting out the vote.

The most complicated campaign is, of course, the one for the Presidency. It is, in fact, not one campaign, but hundreds with the same objective. The candidate's personal advisers conduct the major campaign with the help of their party's national committee. Meanwhile the state, county, and local parties campaign for the national ticket and for their own candidates. As you have seen, groups outside the parties also may campaign, including political clubs, citizens' committees, and various pressure groups.

A staff of experts can be very important to a candidate. But he cannot hope to succeed without a large number of volunteer workers to help him with the countless details of a campaign, such as address-

ing envelopes, tacking up posters, passing out literature, organizing rallies, raising money, and going from door to door to ask for votes.

The political clubs and the precinct workers handle such tasks. So do a great many people who usually are not active in politics but want to do what they can to help a candidate win. In the busiest election years there are over six million volunteer workers.

These include thousands of young people not yet old enough to vote, such as the high-school students below who helped Terry Sanford run for Governor of North Carolina and the boy in the adjoining picture who helped Howard Baker become a United States Senator from Tennessee. If you are interested in working in a campaign, talk with one of the party leaders in the precinct where you live or contact a candidate or his local headquarters.

One of the first things a candidate and his advisers must do is estimate how much his campaign is likely to cost. Then they must decide how to pay for it. If there are a small number of voters to reach, there may be very few expenses. But if advertising, television, printing, postage, travel, and salaries are involved, the cost can be high.

Mrs. Rowan Boone's race for town council cost $1,500. Ralph Chandler's campaign for Congress came to $32,000. These may seem like large sums, but they are far less than what many candidates spend. Campaigning for a seat in the House of Representatives, for example, often costs over $50,000. The cost of a campaign for governor ranges from about $100,000 in a state with a small population to several million dollars in New York and California. A Presidential campaign is still more expensive, with costs of $15 million or more not unusual.

From where does the money come? If a candidate is wealthy, he may pay for a campaign himself, spending whatever he feels is necessary. Far more often he must rely on contributions from individuals and from organizations, particularly business groups and labor unions. How much he raises determines how much he can spend. Mr. Chandler received over 600 contributions, ranging from a few dollars to $2,000. Most people gave because they admired him or felt more Republicans in Congress would be desirable. A few hoped their contribution would entitle them to special treatment if he were elected.

Mr. Chandler also received money from various Republican Party groups, such as the state committee and the Congressional Campaign Committee. In addition, party organizations in the counties in which he campaigned sponsored fund-raising dinners like the one above.

Such affairs are one of the most widely used methods of raising money for campaigns, with "guests" paying from a few dollars to $500 as an admission fee. All regular party workers and persons for whom the party has done favors are expected to attend.

Still more money may be raised through bake sales, coffee and cocktail parties, sales of campaign buttons, and appeals by mail and over TV.

With a President to elect and candidates for Congress to help, the national parties are the busiest fund raisers of all. Millions of persons each year receive a letter like the one below from one of the major parties asking them to contribute $10. Wealthy persons are asked to give far more. In addition, for a membership fee of $1,000, they may join special clubs through which they can meet high officials,

RAY C. BLISS
*Chairman, Republican
National Committee*

NATIONAL
SUSTAINING PROGRAM
for
REPUBLICAN PARTY HEADQUARTERS
1625 EYE STREET, N.W. • WASHINGTON, D.C.

LUCIUS D. CLAY
*Chairman, Republican
Finance Committee*

Dear Fellow American:

"We can't afford to muff the opportunity of 1968." That's the sentiment expressed over and over again by Republicans here in Washington...and it's probably the view of your GOP friends, too.

That's why I've put this letter to you high on my list of priority projects. I would be remiss if I didn't invite you to become a Sustaining Member of Republican Headquarters -- for just $10 -- in this important pre-election year.

Your support can help the GOP recapture the reins of our nation's destiny ...move the country another giant step toward re-establishing two party government...and get the government back on some sensible system of financing and spending.

The Democrat budget calls for expenditures of $370 million every day in the year...$15.4 million every hour! Spending at this rate staggers the imagination. But it's even worse when you consider what it means in terms of your annual tax bite.

If you are like most Americans, your biggest expense every year is the federal income tax. Yet your payment slips through the government's fingers in a twinkling of an eye. And taxes will go even higher if we don't bring a halt to this fiscal extravagance.

The only hope is for Republicans to join forces, to strengthen the Party from top to bottom and push forward from the success already attained Sustaining Fund is vital to laying the f state and a including the President, attend "briefings" on national problems, and be invited to fancy parties. In a recent year there were 5,000 members of such clubs. Their membership fees came to $5 million.

It is important to remember, however, that most political contributions are very small. One of the great weaknesses of our political system, in fact, is that not enough people contribute to the candidate or party they favor. At best only one adult in ten does.

Another difficulty is that the cost of campaigning is rising rapidly. As a result it often is hard for a candidate to obtain all the money he needs unless he is wealthy or turns to persons and organizations willing to make large contributions. The problem is that some expect favors in return. This is not always true, but it happens often enough to discourage many able men and women from running for office. There are laws regulating just how much a candidate may spend and how much individuals and organizations may give, but unfortunately they are not well enforced.

JOHN LINDSAY

Candidate for Mayor

promises:

"The #2 Bus
will run on 7th Avenue
every 10 minutes when
I am Mayor."

ON NOVEMBER 2
ELECT LINDSAY MAYOR

John Lindsay speaks on Crime and Safety

"New York is a city afraid. We're afraid to walk our streets, afraid to play in our parks, afraid to ride in our subways, and even afraid behind the locked doors of our own homes.

"In our city there is a murder every 14 hours, a reported rape every six hours; a reported assault every 12 minutes; a reported theft every three minutes. In ten years our city's crime rate has jumped 33 per cent. In the past year alone, major crimes skyrocketed almost 15 per cent.

"This increasing lawlessness, and the terror it creates, cannot be tolerated.

"We <u>must</u> make our city safe again for all our people, no matter the cost, no matter the effort. I promise it will be done.

"We will institute Operation Safe City, a sweeping around-the-clock war on crime, which will include:

● A massive patrol: doubling police cars, tripling motorcycles.

(over)

When John Lindsay and his advisers planned his campaign for Mayor of New York, they decided he would make two points in his speeches and publicity. First, he would emphasize his plans to solve the many problems that affected everyday life in the city, such as the high crime rate and the poor bus service. Second, he would attack his opponent, Abraham Beame, as a member of a political machine

49

that had done nothing for the city in 20 years. As the Lindsay organization saw it, these were the issues that would attract the greatest interest and the most votes.

Every candidate must make a similar decision on the issues he is going to stress. Usually these concern the way the government has

THE MYTH OF BEAME'S RECORD

There are two Beames. One is a candidate. The other was a high-ranking city official for twenty years. Each has a record. Candidate Beame makes promises, but city official Beame has already acted. When he had the power, city official Beame voted....

1. Against Education

He consistently voted against raising teachers' salaries...against improving schools...against the recommendations of the Board of Education. Today, when nationwide tests reveal our children lag behind the entire nation in reading and writing, Beame is still bragging that we have more public schools than the entire State of Connecticut. Where was Beame's vision on education?

2. Against Public Safety

Beame consistently voted against modernizing the police methods, against releasing patrolmen for street duty, against more patrol cars, against centers to combat juvenile delinquency and the narcotics problem... programs he advocates today. Where was his vision as the crime rate climbed to alarming heights and people began bolting themselves indoors at night?

3. Against Hospitals

Beame has voted against modernizing hospitals, against hiring badly-needed nurses, against the construction of new buildings. As our hospitals deteriorated, as the medical authorities warned of pending disaster, where was Beame's vision?

4. Against Air Pollution Controls and Water Conservation

Beame voted against plans for air pollution controls, despite the warnings by city commissioners. As the water crisis developed, Beame continued to sell city-owned watershed lands. Is this the kind of vision we want in a Mayor?

5. Against Sound Fiscal Planning

Despite claims of his fiscal ability, New York City today is nearly bankrupt because of incredibly poor fiscal planning. That's what the experts say. Every civic organization that knows anything about the city has recommended a long-range fiscal plan, but Beame has consistently and mysteriously opposed this good-government action. On the sales tax, city official Beame successfully urged increasing it until he became candidate Beame.

He did, however, manage to vote increases in the salaries of the political and clubhouse leaders on the city payroll. Is this the vision we want in a Mayor?

6. Against Investigations and Good Government

Beame had the power and the duty to investigate the major and the petty corruptions that plague this city and demoralize New Yorkers. He used that power only once — to investigate the World's Fair, this year. He also insists that district leaders will remain on the city payroll in key positions, thus blocking effective municipal reform. Is this the vision we want in a Mayor?

AS A POWERFUL CITY OFFICIAL, BEAME HAS FAILED TO UNDERSTAND THE PROBLEMS OF EDUCATION, OF CRIME, OF MEDICAL SERVICES, OF AIR POLLUTION, OF WATER, OF TAXES, AND OF CORRUPTION.

HE UNDERSTANDS THE CARE AND FEEDING OF MACHINE POLITICIANS, BUT THAT'S NOT HOW TO RUN A CITY IN CRISIS.

FOR THE DOCUMENTED STORY, TURN THE PAGE....

been run, problems the people have, or the rival candidate and his qualifications. When Lyndon Johnson ran for President against Barry Goldwater, he claimed Mr. Goldwater's proposals would get us into a major war if he were elected. When John Kennedy ran for President against the Republican Richard Nixon, he concentrated his fire on how the Republicans had been handling the government, claiming there had been no progress, urging it was time to get the country moving again.

There are many important subjects to discuss in any campaign, but usually a candidate will stress two or three that enable him to make the strongest arguments against his opponent. In a major campaign, researchers may be used to find out which issues concern the voters most. They also may carefully check the records of the other candidates to determine if they said or did anything in the past that could be used against them. The Lindsay researchers checked Mr. Beame's record as a city official in this way. Then Mr. Lindsay used what they learned to warn how bad things would be if his opponent were elected. Meanwhile, Mr. Beame was attacking Mr. Lindsay's background.

The campaign that is most useful to voters is one in which each candidate discusses all the major issues. When the issues are dramatic and seriously affect the voter, the candidate with the best arguments and programs often is the winner. In other cases the issues may not have too much to do with who is elected. Instead a man may win because he is the better speaker or is better known or because he has a better personality, a better organization, more money, or even better advertising.

In the Presidential election of 1840 it was advertising and publicity more than anything else that gave the Whig Party its first major victory as General William Henry Harrison, hero of the Battle of Tippecanoe, and his running mate, John Tyler, won over the Democrats. The Whigs did not have a single issue of importance. They had not even bothered to develop a platform at their convention. But they did have other advantages.

One was a memorable slogan: "Tippecanoe and Tyler, too." Another was a symbol—a miniature log cabin with a barrel of hard cider in front, like the one above—to show what down-to-earth fellows the candidates really were. Still another was a lively song that began:

"Now the Whigs at the coming election will carry our candidates through;
* They've made the judicious selection of Tyler and Tippecanoe...."*

Four years later the Whigs tried again, this time with Henry Clay and Theodore Frelinghuysen. They went around with badges like the one to the right, and sang:

"Hurrah, hurrah, the country's risin' for Henry Clay and Frelinghuysen."

Sad to say, they lost. Even sadder to say, campaign songs no longer are very important. However, there *is* a great deal of advertising and publicity. At least half the money spent for political campaigns in this country is for this purpose.

Preparations for advertising usually are made well before a campaign gets under way. In local races volunteers often make the arrangements. When higher offices are at stake, an advertising agency or a publicity firm is likely to be hired. One of the first tasks is creating a slogan to be used over and over again. Some slogans express the main idea of a campaign, such as "Peace with Honor" and "Experience Counts." Others simply are easy to remember, like "Keep Cool with Coolidge," "Win with Willkie," and "LBJ for the USA."

Next, the advertising itself must be prepared, then scheduled for use in the best places and at the most effective times. This may involve ads for newspapers, magazines, and billboards, like the one above, as well as commercials for radio and television. In his campaign for Congress, Ralph Chandler relied heavily on radio announcements that were concentrated during those hours when people were driving to and from work. Candidates with more money make heavy use of television. Here is a hard-hitting TV commercial that was used throughout the country in Lyndon Johnson's campaign against Barry Goldwater. Some people regarded it as unfair. What do you think?

54

This girl is picking petals off a daisy.

As she counts them one by one…

a voice in the background begins a countdown. When the voice reaches zero…

the girl is replaced on the screen by a nuclear explosion. Then Mr. Johnson's voice is heard. "These are the stakes…

To make a world in which God's children can live…or go into the dark. We must either love each other or we must die…

VOTE FOR PRESIDENT JOHNSON ON NOVEMBER 3.

The stakes are too high for you to stay home."

Posters also are used to spread the word about a candidate, as they have been since the early days of our country.

Buttons also are used for this purpose.

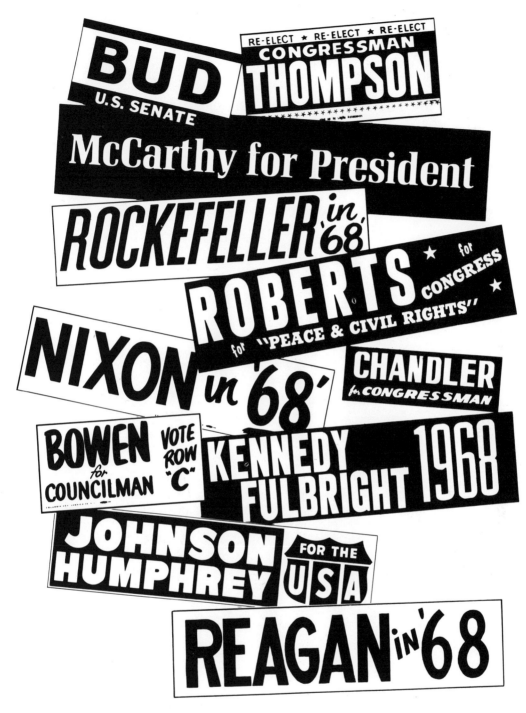

So are bumper stickers and brochures.

And so are balloons that carry a candidate's name, like these Charles Weltner of Atlanta is giving away in his campaign for Congress. And so are canes, combs, fans, key chains, pens, potholders, and thimbles.

By early September the campaigning has begun in earnest as candidates speak their minds at factory gates, shopping centers, and country fairs, in meeting halls and living rooms, on street corners, at great rallies, and on radio and television. Often a campaign is colorful and exciting, but for a candidate constantly on the move, making hundreds of speeches, it can be grueling.

Mr. Chandler's campaign for Congress began each day at dawn when he stood outside a factory gate in one of the four counties he was trying to cover and shook hands with workers. It ended 16 hours later with a speech in a meeting hall somewhere. When Warren Wilentz ran for United States Senator in New Jersey, he had an en-

tire state to reach and, like many candidates, used a helicopter to get around. When Richard Nixon ran for President against John Kennedy, he campaigned in every state, traveling 75,000 miles in seven weeks. The first day was typical. He spoke in Baltimore, then flew by chartered jet to Indianapolis, Dallas, and San Francisco.

But a candidate cannot go everywhere. If his time is to be used wisely, he must campaign where there is a chance of winning the greatest number of votes. If a city, a county, or even a state appears to be solidly for or against him, usually it receives far fewer visits than places in which important gains are possible. Where the candidate is going to appear, often careful arrangements must be made. There must be a place to speak, an audience to hear him, a speech on issues that mean something in the area, and newsmen to report what he says so that a still larger audience will be reached.

In the early days candidates for office also did a lot of traveling, but they moved about on horseback or by carriage, stagecoach, or riverboat. When they arrived at the place they were to speak, they would stand on a tree stump or some other raised area and their audience would gather around them, as in this painting by George Caleb Bingham. As a result, campaigning in one place after another became known as "stumping." Although stumping was widespread, curiously most Presidential candidates neither stumped nor campaigned in any other way. Instead they remained quietly at home while their supporters tried to win votes for them.

Toward the end of the 19th century, however, Presidential candidates began to speak out. This is William McKinley, the Republican candidate in 1896, campaigning from his front porch in Canton, Ohio. Although he did little or no traveling, special trains brought hundreds of thousands of supporters to Canton to hear him discuss his ideas.

But McKinley's opponent William Jennings Bryan did travel. Bryan was the first politician to campaign throughout the country. He covered 18,000 miles that year, speaking from the platform of a special train as it paused in hundreds of towns, or "whistle stops," along the railroad. "Whistle-stopping" soon became one of the most important ways of campaigning. It still is used occasionally, although now there are faster and easier ways to reach the voters.

The man above is Theodore Roosevelt who ran for President in 1904 as a Republican and won, and ran again in 1912 as a third-party candidate and lost. His advice to other candidates still is carefully followed: "Let the audience see you smile...." For his audience to *hear* him, however, he had to shout as loudly as he could since there were no microphones in his day. It was not until the 1920's that they became available.

It also was in the 1920's that candidates began campaigning over the radio, for the first time reaching millions of voters. One of the best radio campaigners was Theodore's cousin, President Franklin Roosevelt.

This is Cadillac Square in Detroit where, on Labor Day, Democratic candidates for President traditionally make their first major campaign speech. The candidate is John Kennedy. "Give me your help, your hand, and your vote," he cries, "and this country can move again!" The crowd of 60,000 roars. Rallies like this go back to 1840 when the supporters of "Tippecanoe and Tyler, too" came together by the thousands to urge on their heroes.

Political parades also are an American tradition. The one shown took place in 1860 in New York as part of Abraham Lincoln's campaign for President. The group parading was known as the Republican Wide-Awakes. They wore shiny black hats and capes, carried torches, and marched in cities all over the North. Sometimes such parades were miles long. Today's political parade usually is a parade of cars in which a candidate is driven through a city to let the voters see him.

For every major rally and every glamorous parade there are thousands of occasions when a candidate speaks from the back of a truck or from a street corner with only a handful of people for an audience, as United States Senator Robert Taft did when he stumped for re-election in Ohio.

Candidates also campaign on foot, shaking hands with the people they meet, listening to their problems, then asking for their votes. Here Nelson Rockefeller walks through a Puerto Rican neighborhood in New York as he campaigns for governor.

A candidate often goes to great lengths to demonstrate for the voters and the photographers how friendly and agreeable he is.

He may, for example, wear a dashing sombrero…

or try his luck, and his wife's luck, in a dogsled race…

or interrupt a busy schedule to play with a pretty baby or do anything else within reason if people will think well of him for it.

But it is not always so pleasant in a campaign. In the 1964 race for President, Barry Goldwater was called a "fool," a "frustrated dictator," and a "victim of a nervous breakdown." His opponent Lyndon Johnson was called a "cheat," a "phony," and "a coddler of Communists." Such attacks are nothing new in politics. Jefferson was called a "drunkard"; Lincoln, "a ghoul"; Theodore Roosevelt, a "trigger-happy maniac." However, often, more than name-calling is involved. Each year millions of pieces of literature are distributed that contain dreadful insults and outright lies regarding candidates.

One of the earliest examples is the handbill decorated with coffins shown below. It accuses Andrew Jackson of the execution of innocent soldiers under his command when, in fact, they had been shot for mutiny or desertion.

One of the most outrageous campaign lies in recent times involved the photograph above. It was used to help defeat Senator Millard Tydings of Maryland when he ran for reelection. His opponent's supporters claimed that Mr. Tydings was a Communist sympathizer. As proof they produced the photograph which shows him listening to a Communist leader. The picture had been created by pasting photographs of the two men next to each other.

What is done about such tactics? An organization called the Fair Campaign Practices Committee fights them as best it can. However, thoughtful citizens can do a great deal on their own. They can ignore name-calling, reject attacks based on racial or religious prejudice, and demand solid proof for other accusations.

One of the best means of judging two or more rivals for office is a "candidates' meeting" at which each candidate speaks on the same issue, then answers questions from the voters present. This man is addressing such a meeting in St. Petersburg, Florida. Not all cities and towns have candidates' meetings, but hundreds are sponsored each year by civic organizations like the League of Women Voters.

Some candidates also debate the issues on television and radio. Over 100 million people watched at least one of the four debates between John Kennedy and Richard Nixon in the 1960 Presidential campaign. Up to that point the most famous political debates were those between Abraham Lincoln and Stephen A. Douglas in 1858 when the two campaigned for United States Senator from Illinois. Unfortunately many candidates are unwilling to participate in a debate or a candidates' meeting, fearing they might lose more votes than they could hope to gain.

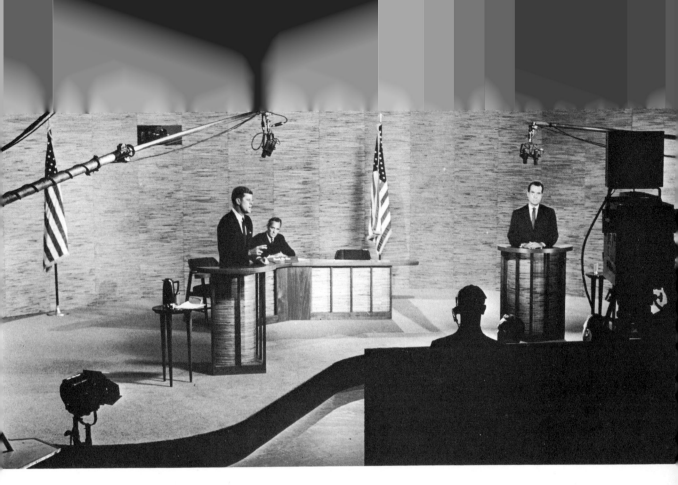

77

A candidate not only seeks the support of individual voters but of organizations that can help him win votes. Labor unions are one of the most important sources of such backing. They interview candidates, study their opinions and records, and then support those men and women they believe would be of most help in advancing their programs. When a union decides to back a candidate, it often distributes handbills urging his election, contributes money to his campaign, and works to get its members to the polls on Election Day. As we have discussed, business, farm, and veterans' organizations and other groups also may help candidates who can help them.

There are, in addition, two other kinds of support that can be useful. One is the endorsement of a newspaper, which usually is announced in an editorial. The other is the endorsement of an important man. When Ralph Chandler ran for Congress, he had the backing of former President Eisenhower, who posed with him for the photograph below. It then was sent to every newspaper in Mr. Chandler's area.

Nation Needs Senator Case

Sen. Clifford P. Case is one of the most able, energetic and articulate men ever to represent New Jersey in the legislative halls in Washington.

His experience in Washington has been in both legislative bodies. He was elected five times to the House of Representatives. New Jersey first named him to the Senate in 1954. His record was so good that New Jersey elected him again in 1960.

Sen. Case is coming back to the people now to ask for a third term.

We believe wholeheartedly that Sen. Case should continue in Washington in the difficult years ahead. Our state needs him there. He adds daily to our state's prestige. But, more important, the whole nation needs Sen. Case—and, truly, others like him —for guidance and leadership.

Sen. Case is a liberal Republican. He has been characterized by opponents within the part~ Democrat masquerading as a P~ ~

This alleg~~

S~ ~

In the early days of our country only a few people could vote. These were men who were at least 21 years old. They had white skin, could read and write, owned enough property to pay a large tax, and had lived in their areas for a certain period. Only 6 white men in every 100 qualified.

Today there are far fewer qualifications for voting. They include age (as low as 18 in some states), length of time in an area (often 1 year in a state, 6 months in a county, 30 days in a precinct), and the ability to read and write. As a result, most of the nation's adults are qualified to vote—over 120 million, in all.

But over 30 million of these still cannot cast ballots. This is because they have not registered with election officials and therefore are not listed as voters. Almost every state requires that its citizens register so that persons who are not qualified to vote can be kept from doing so.

The large number of unregistered voters is a special problem for the Democratic Party, since 7 such persons in 10 are likely to back its candidates. If more were registered, the Democrats might win more elections. At times the Republicans are in the same situation.

As a result, workers from both parties conduct registration drives among people who might support them. Labor unions also conduct

such drives among their members. By examining registration records and knocking on doors, workers find out who is not registered in a neighborhood, then help them to do so.

Some people don't register because they don't know it is necessary. Others don't care enough to take the trouble. And often it *is* trouble. In many states voters can register only on certain days and at hours that may not be convenient for someone who works. At times they must travel to another town to register. If they move or do not vote for a certain period, they may have to register again. Frequently it is easier to get a fishing license than it is to register. However, officials in some areas are working to improve the situation by setting up special neighborhood centers to register voters where they live or work. This mobile registration unit in Denver is an example.

These people in Canton, Mississippi, are registering to vote a few days after the Voting Act of 1965 became law. Although Negroes have had the right to register and vote for over a century, unfair regulations have kept them from doing so in many sections of the South. The law changed this. If local officials will not register someone who is qualified, then a Federal official, such as the man in the photograph, will do it. Since the law went into effect hundreds of thousands of Negroes have registered for the first time. Suddenly they have become important to politicians in search of votes.

83

Early in November the speeches, the parades, the handshaking finally come to an end, and the people go to the polls to make their decision. Voter after voter enters a booth and casts his ballot. It all is done so quickly and so easily we tend to forget that the right to vote and thereby govern ourselves was bought at a great price. In recent years the Negro has risked jail and injury—even death—so that he could vote. Earlier, the nation's women fought against overwhelming odds until in 1920 they finally gained this right. In many other areas of the world the struggle for self-government still goes on.

Not all Americans use their vote, however. In a Presidential race about 7 adults in 10 cast ballots. In a Congressional contest often less than half do. In a local election frequently only 1 in 5 may vote. It is the youngest voters, those from 18 to 25, who have the poorest voting records. On the other hand, there are people who vote in ignorance, basing their decisions on a candidate's personality or on appeals he has made to emotion and prejudice rather than on his qualifications and the issues. This is just as bad as not voting.

As the political parties see it, however, every vote counts. They have learned through hard experience that a few votes can sometimes make the difference in an election. In recent years, for example, a governor of Rhode Island was elected by 398 votes and a governor of Minnesota by 91. As a result of such situations, workers may spend all of Election Day getting as many of "their" voters as possible to the polls.

Some have the job of hanging reminders on doorknobs, like the woman above in Chicago. Others may baby-sit so that mothers of young children can vote. Still others may serve as drivers, taking people to vote who don't have transportation of their own. Meanwhile, workers at the polls keep track of who has not voted and either send someone to fetch them or have them called on the telephone.

Usually each party also will have challengers or poll watchers at a voting place. The man and the two women at the right in the picture on Page 84 have this job. Their task is to make sure that only eligible voters are voting and that the votes are tallied correctly. Dishonesty is no longer the problem it was in the early 1900's when registration lists often were padded with the names of people who had moved away or died and others were paid to vote as if they were these persons. But even today a dishonest election official may try to cast extra votes on a voting machine or, where paper ballots are used, try to spoil votes for a man he opposes so that they cannot be counted. As a result, it is important to be on guard.

By early evening the last votes have been cast, the polls are closed, and the counting begins.

Candidates for local offices may know if they have won or lost in a matter of minutes. For others there is a longer wait. To get a picture of how the election is going, they may meet with their advisers, talk by telephone with workers in important areas, and keep close track of radio and TV reports. Usually these are the most helpful.

87

With newsmen calling in the results from key polling places and a computer to do the arithmetic, a TV network may know the outcome of an election within an hour or two.

In the closest races, however, far more time may be involved. Although John Kennedy had a good lead over Richard Nixon at midnight, it was not until the next morning, after most of the votes had been counted, that he knew for certain he would be President.

For months a man may give all of himself to a campaign, and so may people who believe in him. If he loses, as Barry Goldwater did in his campaign for President, there is deep disappointment.

If he wins, as Edward Brooke of Massachusetts did in his race for United States Senator, there is unrestrained joy.

But an election victory is a beginning, not an end. The chance to serve that the winner sought lies ahead. How successful he is depends in large part on him and on the difficulties he faces. However, a voter also has a duty. It is keeping this man or woman who now represents him aware of his views: what he sees as the problems, what he thinks the solutions might be. Without this help no officeholder can do his job as well as he might.

Yet even with an election barely over, with men and women starting their terms in office, others already are thinking about the next election, wondering about who might run, what his chances might be, what *their* chances might be.

92

Terms Used in an Election Campaign

Boss. See Page 22.

Caucus. A meeting of party leaders or convention delegates to plan strategy. Also, an official party meeting at which candidates are nominated.

Chairman. See Pages 20, 21.

Challenger. See Page 86.

Citizens' Organization. See Pages 23, 40.

Committee. See Pages 20, 21.

Constituents. The persons an officeholder represents.

Convention. See Pages 25–38.

Dark Horse. A little-known person who obtains a nomination for office because it is felt he can be elected or will make a good showing.

Draft. A situation in which convention delegates insist someone accept a nomination he does not want. In such cases, a person is "drafted" to run.

Election Clerks, Judges. Persons appointed to supervise voting at a polling place.

Election District. See Page 20.

Electoral Voting. The system by which the President and Vice President are chosen. Each state has the same number of electoral votes as it has Senators and Representatives in Congress. The candidate who gets the largest vote from the state's citizens wins all the state's electoral votes. Some 269 are needed for election. The *electors* who cast the electoral votes in each state make up what is known as the *Electoral College.* There have been many efforts to replace this system. The major reason is that a party's candidate for President and Vice President may win a majority of the electoral votes, yet get only a minority of the citizens' votes. This has happened at least 11 times in our history.

Grass Roots. The local level.

Incumbent. Someone who already holds office.

Independent. See Pages 18, 19.

Issue. A subject for debate in a campaign. See Pages 49–51.

Leader. See Pages 20, 21.

Machine. See Page 22.

Marginal Seat. See Seat.

Political Club. See Page 23.

Political Organization. See Pages 21, 22.

Political Party. See Pages 12–22.

Patronage. Jobs and other favors that a party controlling a government may give its supporters.

Platform. See Page 31.

Plurality. The number of votes separating a winning candidate from the one who finishes second.

Poll Watcher. See Page 86.

Precinct. See Page 20.

Primary Election. See Pages 25–29.

Registered Voter. See Pages 80–83.

Running Mate. Usually a candidate for the second-highest office. For example, a candidate for Vice President is the running mate of the candidate for President.

Seat. A membership in a state legislature or some other lawmaking body. A *marginal seat* is a membership for which there will be a close contest. A *safe seat* is a membership a party is not in danger of losing.

Slate. See Ticket.

Smoke-Filled Room. A reference to a meeting of powerful politicians who make decisions, then impose them on their party. The smoke usually is cigar smoke.

Split Ticket. See Ticket.

Straight Ticket. See Ticket.

Stumping. See Pages 62, 63.

Swing Area. A county or some other area that does not repeatedly vote for the same party.

Ticket. All the candidates a party selects to run in an election. Also known as a slate. A person who votes a *straight ticket* votes for all of a party's candidates. A voter who votes a *split ticket* votes for candidates from more than one party.

Ward. See Page 20.

Ward Heeler. A person who serves a political boss.

Acknowledgments

I am grateful to the following individuals and organizations for their generous help with the research for *The People's Choice*.

Office of United States Senator Howard H. Baker, Jr.; Business-Industry Political Action Committee; The Boatmen's National Bank of St. Louis; Geraldine Boone; Office of United States Senator Edward Brooke; Citizens' Research Foundation, Herbert E. Alexander; Columbia Broadcasting System; The Reverend Ralph Chandler; AFL-CIO Committee on Political Education, Benjamin Albert; William Deitz; Democratic Congressional Campaign Committee, Ken Harding; Democratic National Committee, Billie Farnum, Albert Mark, Whyche Fowler; Doyle Dane Bernbach, James Graham; Fair Campaign Practices Committee, Sam Archibald, Patricia Young; George Gallup, Jr.; Jack Gleason; Joseph Goeke; *Hunterdon County Democrat* (N.J.), Edward Mack; *Hunterdon Review*, Grace Clark; Joseph Katz; League of Women Voters of the United States; *Life* magazine; National Association of Manufacturers, William Stoltze.

Also, National Broadcasting Company, Joseph Riccuiti; New Jersey State Democratic Committee, Byron Charoff, Fred Sacco; *Phillipsburg Free Press* (N.J.), Taylor Holbrook; Republican Congressional Campaign Committee, William Theis; Republican National Committee, Ab Hermann, John Hunger, Gus Miller, Fred Morrison; Office of United States Senator Margaret Chase Smith; Smithsonian Institution, Keith Melder, Philip Brooke; United States Representative Frank Thompson, Jr.; *The Trenton Times* (N.J.), Chamber of Commerce of the United States of America, Dorothy Fleckner, Robert Sneure; Mr. and Mrs. Robert Worcester.

ALVIN SCHWARTZ

Princeton, New Jersey

Illustration Credits

When more than one illustration appears on a page, the letter "A" next to the page reference indicates a top or left position and the letter "B" indicates a bottom or right position.

AFL-CIO Committee on Political Education (courtesy): 41, 78, 81A & B, 85

Baker, United States Senator Howard (courtesy): 43

Black Star: photo by Gene Daniels, 34; photo by Steve Shapiro, 36A; *St. Louis Post-Dispatch*, 71

Boatmen's National Bank of St. Louis: painting by George Caleb Bingham, 63

Brown Brothers: 17, 22A & B, 77B

Chandler, The Reverend Ralph (courtesy): photos by T. Myndyllo, 45. 46, 79

Democratic National Committee (courtesy): 11A (Lyndon Johnson), 21, 23, 42

Doyle Dane Bernbach Inc. (courtesy): 55

Granger Collection: painting by John Trumbull, 12A; painting by Rembrandt Peale, 12B

Harris & Ewing: 67

Hunterdon County Democrat: 11B

League of Women Voters (courtesy): 24, 76

Library of Congress: 14, 15, 30B, 56A

Magnum: photos by Cornell Capa, 39, 87

Monkmeyer: photos by Sybil Shelton, frontis, 10, 84

National Broadcasting Company (courtesy): 30A, 35B, 36B, 77A, 88, 89

Nebraska State Historical Society: 65

New Jersey State Democratic Committee: *The Trenton Times*, 62

The New York Times: 92

Rocky Mountain News: photo by Mel Shieltz, 82

Smithsonian Institution: 52, 53, 56B, 57A & B, 64, 66, 69A, 74

United Press International: 16A & B, 28, 54, 68, 69B, 70, 72A (Adlai Stevenson). 72B (George Romney), 75, 83, 90

Wide World: 29, 31, 33, 35A, 37, 38, 60, 73 (Hubert Humphry), 91

Worcester, Mr. & Mrs. Robert (courtesy): 58